PICKING UP THE PIECES

By

Yolanda Roary

Copyright © 2021 by Yolanda Roary

The scanning, uploading, copying, or distribution of this book without permission from the Author is prohibited. For permission to use this book (other than for review purposes), please contact admin@totalgraceconsulting.org

Thank you for your support of the author's rights.

Yolanda Roary, Total Grace Consulting

ISBN: 978-0-578-85890-6

Printed in the United States of America

Table of Contents

Chapter One: A Daddy's Role 5

Chapter Two: The Mother in Me 7

Chapter Three: Before Goodbye 9

Chapter Four: The Empty Inside of Emptiness 11

Chapter Five: The Man in the Mirror 15

Chapter Six: This is my Exodus 25

Chapter Seven: Your Present Suffering 30

Chapter Eight: God Meets Us Where We Are 34

Chapter Nine: Release is the Prerequisite to Restoration 38

Chapter Ten: The Threshing of the Wheat 42

Chapter Eleven: The Dry Wood Factor 44

Chapter Twelve: Choose the Mandate and Not the Mess 46

Chapter Thirteen: The Transformation 50

Chapter Fourteen: Broken to keep Breaking 52

Chapter Fifteen: The Beginning of a New Ending 57

Thank you

The journey of picking up the broken pieces in your life will never end. Each test, trial, and tribulation will breed brokenness in some way, shape, or form. Our job is to recognize the brokenness and accept Gods way of mending or destroying the thing that broke us. During this journey, I would not have made it without some very important people in my life. I say THANK YOU!

To my husband, Maurice, I love you with a Godly love. Thank you for being the man of God that you are. Thank you for trusting the God in me to share parts of our journey that others may be saved and delivered. Your unwavering faith and determination to stand for God, despite your challenges, downfalls, and mistakes has made you the great man that you are. I commend you for not giving up on me or our family. You chose to lay aside every weight that would take you away from God's ordained order for our marriage, and for that I say thank you. The love you give, your selfless acts of kindness, and your immeasurable push is simply amazing. I honor you today. May you continually be used of God and be an example for men across the world, of the work God is able to do.

To my children, thank you for enduring as God delivered me.

To my Pastor, Dr. Lopez.......I could not ask for a better spiritual mother. You've taught me to STAND, you taught me to walk on water and ride the waves of life. You are a living example of the tangible of GOD and the woman I consider to be the angel assigned to my life by GOD. Thank you for being a great shepherd.

To Sonya and Crystal, you are dry wood to the fire in my life.

To my mom and grandmother, thank you for being patient with me during my silent place in God. I know you didn't understand, but God was making me a better woman.

Shelly, your prayer and guidance in this process will never be forgotten.

To Elder Bates....yes, I learned how to love!

To my sissy Tina, I can always count on you to help me release my frustration in fun ways.

Letroy and Christina (Married 4Real) thank you for your mentorship, your direction, and accountability.

Preface

Through Christ I have learned that I must accept, adjust, and acquire. Accept the right and wrong. Adjust to the emotion behind it and acquire the good that is hidden beneath it.

Life is full of lessons to be learned and actions to be taken. Behaviors, positions, and environments teach us the good, bad and ugly. Life holds the capacity to teach us where we belong in organizations, systems, and in the lives of others. Sometimes the lesson will hurt. My experience did not feel good, but it was for my good. It was piercing to the soul. I ask the question, what will you do with the pain, and your broken pieces? Will you take the opposition and allow it to become opportunity for elevation, or will the pain make you bitter and resentful? Will the pain shift or sift you?

"Everyone and everything around you is your teacher." - Ken Keyes Jr.

2019 has been full of pain and gain. I have learned to love in-spite of. Live in-spite of, and give grace in-spite of. I am picking up the pieces to a better me. I invite you in as I share my truth. I will share my becoming.

God transformed me by using my broken pieces to shift me from who I was, into the process of who he called me to be. Process, because it is never ending. We are forever in the hands of God and he is forever making, shaping, and molding us.

My process includes every part of who I am, the wife, mother, sister, friend, and daughter...but most of all, The Woman of God He Created. This season of picking up, throwing away, and giving to God, changed my mind, opened my heart, and saved my life.

This book grants you permission to walk with me in a season of hurt, and uncertainty. A season where my reality came alive in me. This is the journey of how I accepted and allowed God's grace to guide me through the valley of dry bones in my life. My pieces were laid out, awaiting my arrival. The pieces were there for years, now dry brittle and breaking. But in order to live, some of them needed to die. To remain buried, to remain distant from my Christian walk. Their presence crippled me, the crutch of the dry bones became a stench of stagnation and death to my destiny. I needed to breathe and live.

Chapter One
A Daddy's Role....

I can remember sleeping on my father's chest at the age of 4 or 5. We were in a small, rectangular bedroom in my grandparent's mobile home. The room was average. The walls were covered with wood paneling (I can see the deer print), a twin bed, and a standard record player/8track combination against the wall. I'm unsure if the box even worked, but I remember it.

The smell of my father's aftershave will never leave me. The peace that came along with being in my daddy's arms, I can feel as I type. Unbeknownst to me, that would be the first and last time I slept in his arms, and the first time I would be welcomed into the arms of rejection, fear, and abandonment I didn't deserve. The first time these emotions would rise up and live inside of me with plans to ruin and destroy my life. It would be years before I saw him again.

As I reveal parts of my life, I will share how the rejection lived in me and how the abandonment made decisions for me. I will also reveal how it was a mirror, reflecting my future. But the mirror doesn't show, how to respond. I had no one in my life familiar with navigating life in a positive way. Dealing with emotion, uncertainty, and pain was easily handled by anger, telling someone how you felt and moving on....but what happens to the root cause? It lies there dormant, waiting on the right opportunity to poke its head and destroy you because no one knew better or did better.

Only God's word and intimacy with a God who never fails, a real daddy, could reveal that and teach you how to walk in his AGAPE Love. After God reveals, you must do the practical work. Study, read, and get counseling, whatever your "work" may be. Find and accept the cure to your ailment.

Picking Up the Pieces............

Chapter Two

The Mother in Me

Although I was raised by a single mother, doing the best she could while raising two girls, she never failed at making sure my sister and I got on the church bus every Sunday morning. She instilled in us the importance of paying our tithes. I can hear her now, "Whatever you do, pay your tithes, and God will take care of you." She was a living, breathing example of how hard a woman will work to ensure her family is taken care of. My sister and I were the apple of our mother's eye.

I will never forget Valentine's Day. Roses and balloons were delivered to our school faithfully. I felt so special! However, I never knew what it felt like to have that from a father. To feel special in his eyes. To feel loved, protected, to feel like a priority.

Now, she has carried on with my grandmother and 4-year-old cousin. She takes care of them, day in and day out. She makes sure they want for nothing. Cooking, cleaning, bathing, everything a mother does. She is the epitome of a caregiver. With everything in her, she makes sure they are well, happy and satisfied.

Momma, I say thank you. You are a legend. I failed to mention, she did not play! If you crossed her, you knew it. In the center console of our white 1977 Oldsmobile Cutlass with a red top was a filleting knife, waiting for the man or woman who pushed one of her buttons.

I grew up with the same cutting spirit. I was not a fighter, but if you crossed me and tears fell, you were bound to be filleted. I think her bold and determined spirit was the hardest thing God had to mold and work out of me. Her determination to never let anyone hurt her again. The brick wall she built up, became the brick wall I built up. The pride and unwillingness to be vulnerable was our life line, it protected us. I was bound for years.

That angry black woman! If an angry black woman lives on the inside of you, deal with her before it's too late. She is a wrecking ball. She has the capacity to ruin your life and the lives attached to you. Your children, spouse, family and friends are at the mercy of her anger, bitterness, rejection, and despair. That rejection, that angry black woman was birthed from an early age in my mom and me as well. Those little girls inside of us were determined to live. Her little girl gained wings of rage after divorcing my dad. She suffered abuse and neglect the short time they were married. As a young girl and woman, I can still feel the displaced anger my mom carried for so long, as I carried it with her.

Looking back at my children and their mistakes, how easy was it to place my anger at their father on them. Too easy. Many times I had to apologize for yelling at them or punishing them when I could have handled things differently. Another piece to be picked up and buried.

Chapter Three
Before Goodbye

I'll never forget the time at the gas station when my dad did not acknowledge me while he was buying candy for someone else's kid. He never apologized for that experience or not being in our lives. That was another brick in my wall, another piece of pride and determination for that little girl to thrive off of. But through God and an awesome boss, I learned that a person cannot give what they don't have, and it's not my responsibility to make them see it or force them to do better. Only God can change someone's heart. It's my job to love. So that's what I did.

After giving birth to my son, my dad and I had several disagreements on his way of life and how I didn't want his habits to ruin my son. The drinking and drugs were a NO and I would not allow my children to be subject to it. If I ever told my dad he could not see, or visit his grandson, you would have thought the world ended!

He spent everyday living to please his grandchildren. He was fully aware that he made a huge mistake not being in my life or my sisters life, and he was determined to make it up through his grandchildren, at all cost. Sick or well, he wanted his "grands", as he called them, near him until the day he died.

Even though daddy lived to please his grandchildren, he did not have an easy life. Daddy understood what it was like to be homeless, what it was like to not have utilities, live on the streets, and hustle to make it. I did not understand it at all. I remember being at his house one Saturday and asking, "Why is this man still here, he stinks!" He said," Pee Wee, everybody needs somebody." In that moment I was humbled and realized that I may be up today but can be down tomorrow just like that man. I repented before God. My dad, a sinner at the time, showed a so-called saint, what the characteristics of God were.

He gave water to the drug dealers across the street when their electricity was turned off. It made me furious, but who am I to judge him or them. My sin stinks in the nostrils of God, just like theirs. I will never forget the lessons learned before he died.

The most glorious moment was the day I walked on his porch and he said, "Pee wee, I have been partying all day, me and Jesus have been dancing up and down the road." I knew he had an encounter with his Heavenly Father. That meant more than anything to know he made peace with GOD.

That following Saturday before he died, I sat beside his bed early that morning and said, "You have been great, and you have nothing left here. Your grandkids love you. You were the best granddad and dad ever. It's ok to go. We love you." That evening he was gone. He left a legacy of family. The legacy taught us that it's never too late to love your family, and right your wrongs. He learned his lesson and showed it through the love he had for his grandchildren.

"You can build where you are broken."

Chapter Four
The Empty Inside of Emptiness

My relationship with my dad and his absence left scars and voids inside of me that bled into my life as a young adult and into my marriage.

Because I had no clue how to deal with the rejection and hurt of my dad's absence, I became very promiscuous at a young age. I lost my virginity at age 13. Did I know what spiritual doors I opened? Was I aware that I had become one with another person? Was I aware that the emotional attachment from one sexual encounter would follow me for years to come? Did I know how to put out the fire I started? NO!

Age at 13, my life changed. That yearning for a man, a feeling, protection, security, the scent of aftershave, it came like a rushing wind. Boyfriend after boyfriend. I made the mistake of opening my spirit, my body, and my heart.

That little girl was lost, wondering in a land of no hope, no justification, no answers, just an uphill journey to feel loved by a man. Another piece to be picked up.

For the first 14 years of my marriage, there was a resounding emptiness inside of me pertaining to my marriage and God. Because of the wounds from my earthly father, I became so consumed with pleasing my husband.

Even though I sang on the praise and worship team, went to Sunday school, and bible study, stayed away from the things that would separate me from Christ (the sin), I became consumed with my husband and not God! I was doing all of the things that I felt were right, but forgetting about the most important thing. GOD! I played the part. I wore the mask, but those with real spiritual discernment saw no God in me. They saw flesh. They saw a woman full of a self she had not denied. I was full of my desire, my hurts, and my wants. Me, me, me, and me some more me. I had no idea that loving God first was the path to loving everyone else. I had no idea that I needed to love a man that I couldn't see (spiritually) before I could love the man that I can see (naturally) the right way. The "man" includes everyone. My husband, children, friends, family, etc.

I was selfish. I lived behind the brick wall my wounds built and I could not see my way out. My wounds spoke and cried out for me. Constantly bleeding on others. The emptiness I felt for my spouse became the emptiness God felt in our relationship. It was a void. All God heard from me was a story of how I was hurt, why was I hurt, and why couldn't I leave the man that hurt me. Have you ever wondered if God feels empty because of your lack of relationship with him?

At year 15, I found a true place in God, true relationship with God and the hurt that I was on the receiving end of no longer controlled me, I controlled it. I was in awe. It was nothing short of a miracle. I was no longer bitter, frustrated, and prideful (at least I thought, read on).

With fasting, prayer, and a deeper call to relationship, God's love covered the hurt, the sting of not being wanted yet again. His love covered every tear, every moment spent beating my head against the bathroom wall, every question, all of it, God's Agape love covered it. With love, I spoke life into the dead bones surrounding my marriage and family.

Don't get it twisted! This was not always easy! When you are fully surrendered, you must allow the joy of the Lord to be your strength in your weakest moments . Then he said unto them, "Go your way, eat the fat, and drink the sweet, and send portions unto them for whom nothing is prepared: for this day is holy unto our Lord: neither be ye sorry; for the joy of the Lord is your strength" (Nehemiah 8:10). There is joy in knowing that you are coming out as pure gold. There is joy in knowing that the battle is already won in Christ Jesus. There is joy in knowing that no weapon formed against me shall prosper. There is joy in knowing that though they slay me, yet will I trust him, boy was the slaying was real! Every rejection, every moment filled with no concern or thought, every place of disrespect. Each one, a new sheep before the slaughter, but it was the same sheep, me. Though he slay me, yet will I trust in him: but I will maintain mine own ways before him (Job 13:15).

Quoting scripture is not easy when everything that you love is falling to pieces. Quote anyway, Pray anyway, Stand anyway!!!! God will carry you! His guidance is never failing and it will lead you into all truth and righteousness. During a test, the teacher is quite. You may be in a season where it seems like God is silent. Just because he is not speaking, doesn't mean he is not there with you. Teaching them to observe all things whatsoever I have commanded you: and lo,

I am with you always, even unto the end of the world. Amen (Matthew 28:20).

Though I failed many times in the process, I was not a failure in the eyes of God. I heard him whisper to me, "I am proud of you, I will take care of you". The love of a father, the peace of a father. To be honest I can't explain it, there are no words that could profoundly articulate God's greatness, but what I can say is ...try him for yourself. Allow him to put you on the potter's wheel. Allow his hands to shape and mold you into your destiny, into what he called you to be.

Chapter Five
The Man in the Mirror
(My story of deliverance)

Our desire for someone else to change has the overwhelming power to make us overlook the change needed in us. God will not show us everyone else, and omit the need for us to see ourselves.

After years of frustration, numbness, wanting to give up, and attitude fueled by bitterness, fear and rejection, and not to mention being a spoiled brat, I began to seek God and ask that he change my husband. Not to mention, I didn't ask this until after all of my attempts failed, attempts without GOD. Well God did just what I asked! When we are united in Holy Matrimony, we become one. So, the change I wanted to see in the man I became one with, took place in me. You cannot love your spouse right, until you love God right. It's impossible. It's Divine Order....God, Your Spouse, Your Children......everyone falls in line after that.

Deliverance requires Exposure (No Saint Here)

God is a restorer! I said it a thousand times. I loved my husband with a new love, a new vision for our marriage, a new vision for our family. I was overflowing with excitement! UNTIL THE EMPTINESS EXCHANGED HANDS.

My husband began to resent me. His heart became hardened, he wanted nothing to do with me. He was present in body, but his heart left a long time ago. He became involved with another woman. I wanted a divorce, and God said NO.

"Love for God will cause you to stay, when everything and everyone else goes astray"

To the floor went my enthusiasm, parts of my faith, pieces of my hope, and pieces of my heart. More pieces needed to be picked up. More work needed to be done. My soul still needed healing, and restoration. It needed to thrive. Our soul is the place where our will and the will of God meets. One must prevail. The will of God is where I wanted and needed to be. I needed practical ways to deal with my pain, but I didn't know it.

In this season, although hard, painful, full of tears, heartaches, sleepless nights, wet pillows, eyelashes falling off, doubtful thoughts, and weary nights, I was able to find strength in God. Despite wiping tears every hour in the bathroom at work, praying and seeing no result, I found strength. It seemed as if matters were getting worse, I found strength.

In this season, I became content with my present state. In this season, the warrior God was preparing by allowing my many afflictions, stood tall, and I couldn't give up even when I wanted to with all inside of me. Not that I speak in respect of want: for I have learned, in whatsoever state I am, to be content (Philippians 4:11).

Picking Up The Pieces

In this season God was my pilot. The love he bestowed into me covered all of the hurt, guilt, shame, accusation, fear, and deceit, but still, I had a soul that needed direction. The practical application, the steps towards dealing with triggers when they were present. Your triggers can be songs, pictures, movies, words, people, places, anything that reminds you of why you were angry, prideful, rejected, and downtrodden. What do you do with those feelings? Compartmentalization was no longer working for me. I needed to remain stable in my faith.

In a dark place, filled with lust, lies, and deceit, God shined His light. The package I wanted delivered from God was not coming the way I expected. In anger, I gave a demand. Either you cut off the communication with her (the other woman) and be with your family or else! Head turning, eyes rolling, and shoulders braced, ready to fight, I told my husband everything going wrong in our marriage and with our children was his fault.

My faults were sitting at the light, waiting on GO! At the right moment and time, God was getting ready to show me who I was. The good, bad and ugly! The exposure God allowed was to expose me. My hate, bitterness, lack of love, and concern, my need to have things my way and control everyone and everything around me, my fairytale marriage was ending when the clock struck 12!

How could this happen, How could he do this to me? In a firm voice, God said, "How could you be so mean and degrading, how could you treat him this way?" REALLY GOD? I CAN DO

BAD ALL BY MYSELF, I DON'T NEED HIM! I said all of that, in that order.

I asked my husband to choose between her and me, and his response was, "I cannot answer that." "WHAT!" "What do you mean?" "It's her or me, period, in that order!" He walked away. I was crushed, bleeding from the inside out. The pain I felt when my dad did not acknowledge me in the store as a child rose up, and this time, tears fell, my heart felt as if it exploded. My life was over, and I had no one to help me put it back together, because the man I dreamed of had walked away. Another man will not hurt me again, played over and over in my head.

That little girl in the store ignored/abandoned by her father was now abandoned again by the man who was to protect her. This time, I couldn't handle it. This time, I broke. God broke every part of me that could break someone else. My prayer was being answered. The prayer to change my husband was happening inside of me. The destruction I faced was needed for the deliverance of my soul. I needed to feel what had been tucked away. God allowed this affair to grace my door, to show me who I was. To show me that I was adulterous towards him, that I had other Gods before him, and that I was not walking in his love. God showed me the root of my deficiency.

Now I knew what needed practical and spiritual application to make me effective in his kingdom. I ran into the bathroom, tears falling, mind shattering, and heart broken. My heart was racing 1,000 beats per minute. My vision was now a blur, I could see nothing in front of me, only clouds that accumulated from tears. As I slid down the wall in grief, my shoulders collapsed along with every part of my being surrendered at that moment. My body, mind, and soul surrendered to God in that place. In that moment, God began to speak, he allowed me to hear every negative word I spoke over my marriage, in my marriage, and to the man I married. He took me back to the place where I inflicted the first word and position of pain in his life.

We had a disagreement, I assumed he was cheating, and I did not give him a chance to speak or explain. I condemned, and that was it. I put him out of my house. Did you catch it? MY HOUSE. Nothing belongs to you. Neither do you have the right to dictate what is yours in a marriage. Everything belongs to the both of you. PERIOD! God said in a gentle voice, "In your selfishness, you made him homeless all over again." (My husband did not have the best childhood, but that's his story to tell). Because of my harshness and lack of desire to LEARN AND SEEK GOD ON HOW TO be a wife, how to recognize the broken parts pieces he carried, I crushed him. To follow, I kept our son away from him on purpose. Did that remind him of the rejection he faced as a child and how he was unable to be a part of his dad's life? How thoughtless and self-centered was I? I didn't think so at all, I was too stubborn to see any of it. My need to "keep it real" was keeping me bound. Until that moment on the floor, until 15 years of my way ended with a phone call. It ended hearing another woman tell me the most secret parts of my husband that he never shared with me, or did he share and I did not listen?

The process of walking down the aisle, the changing of titles from a bride to a wife is easy. Remaining a wife requires discipline, wisdom, humility, and patience. The fruit of the spirit should exude from you after saying I do. "But the fruit of the spirit is love, joy, peace, longsuffering, gentleness, goodness, faith, meekness, temperance: against such there is no law" Galatians 5: 22-23. The fruit of the spirit are a choice. You choose to exude these characteristics; THEY ARE NOT EMOTIONS! If you are not ready to choose them, I suggest you do not get married. "But God hath chosen the foolish things of the world to confound the wise; and God hath chosen the weak things of the world to confound the things which are mighty (1 Corinthians 1:27).

After discovering his affair, I cheated to pay him back. Oh how horrible and disgusting did I feel afterwards! The devil continuously said, "You are stupid, and worth nothing." God forgave me, but I was unable to forgive myself because I couldn't break free from the words of the enemy. Thank God for the woman of God who spoke into my life saying, "God has forgiven you, now forgive yourself."

We must forgive ourselves or we will remain a hostage of the enemy. If he has a chance to get into our minds, he will take control of our lives. And be not conformed to this world: but be ye transformed by the renewing of your mind, that ye may prove what is that good, and acceptable, perfect will of God (Romans 12:2). I fell right into the enemy's trap, I should have allowed God to heal me. I even called the other woman and said, "You can have him, he doesn't have a pot to piss in and a

Picking Up The Pieces

window to throw it out of!" How demeaning to his character was that? The bible tells us to be angry but sin not. My actions were not of God, my intentions were to kill. I allowed my uncontrolled anger, the rage, and the little girl to cause me to sin. I had not dealt with the root of my issue. I had not dealt with seeing a man that I love reject me for someone else. I had not dealt with the father that left me. Repaying evil for evil leaves you bitter and full of resentment. Letting God heal and handle the decision leaves you whole and willing to be a vessel for the kingdom of God. When we decide to cheat on our spouse, we are cheating on God. I never cheated on him again. I learned a valuable lesson.

In the midst of the broken place and atmosphere of sorrow, the voice of God pierced through, and I could hear God calling and speaking. Giving divine direction for my situation. For the steps of a good man are ordered by God: and he delighteth in his way (Psalms 37:23). Pictures are developed in the dark and fulfilled in the light. My dark met its light.

The person you lay down with, now becomes one with you and your spouse. Marriage was created for one man and one woman, not men and women. When you go to a wedding ceremony there are 2 people at the altar, reciting vows, not 3, 4 or 5. Every spirit attached to that person, now dwells with you and your spouse. So you cannot wonder why your spouse is acting differently. They have become joined to someone unequally yoked.

My infidelity caused my husband to become a new man, one I did not know. So when different spirits attached themselves to him, I began to attack him and not the spirit behind the action. Why? Because I invited it in, and had no recollection of what I had done to myself, my husband, or my marriage. We as women are created to respect and honor our husbands. Letroy Brown (Married4Real) states, "A man's heart hears with an ear of respect." Once you find out what respect means to your spouse, (it will vary in every man) ensure that you complete the task as long as it is in the will of God. Marriage is a ministry. A wife is a ministry. You are to minister to the needs of your spouse, daily. Praying for them, more than you complain to them. I ask of you, please do not corrupt your ministry as a wife. The recipe for success is: learn how to serve God, be a wife to him, and you will never fail at serving your spouse. I made a vow to God and kept it, never again did I or will I cheat on my husband!!!!!

I began serving God, so I could serve my husband. Foot massages, back rubs, cooking dinner, date nights, sacrificing my will and desire so that he could be served, honored and respected. Actually listening to him pour out, being concerned with his day to day stress, all of these were reignited in me. I think he was just as shocked as I was, and he probably didn't think it was going to last, but it was real!

In the past, all of this was foreign in our marriage. We adapted functioning inside of dysfunction. We didn't know how to communicate, nothing was on one accord, and we lived in the same house as roommates. We had a sexless marriage for years because of my bitterness. I wanted him to pay for hurting me so I withheld sexual intimacy to punish him.

We can only dwell in darkness for a period of time before Gods correction becomes a tool of exposure and his love becomes the ax that strikes darkness and makes room for the light of God to deliver.

God gave me one word for my husband: **GRACE**

Giving. Receiving. And Caring without Excuse…….

OOOHHH IT HURT TO ACCEPT THAT. I had no way out. I made a commitment and promise, that God commanded me to keep.

Can I **give** when it's not deserved? "It is more blessed to give than receive." (Acts 20:35)

Can I **receive** the bad as I accepted the good? Will the bad change my demeanor, will I show a body language that protrudes what I feel inside, or will I command my mind and body to line up? "Calleth those things which be and not as though they were. " (Romans 4: 17)

Can I **care** when everything inside says walk away? Will my care be without prejudice and carry me to the next place in GOD? "For there is no respect of persons with God" (Romans 2:11)

Can I remove all excuses and rational reasoning without **excuse**? So that my life aligns with Gods will and not my own "For my thoughts are not your thoughts, neither are your ways, saith the Lord." (Isaiah 55:8)

Yolanda Roary

God is not rational, he is right! He does not need to reason with us about anything.

Note: Marriage is not for the weak, and those with no fight inside of them. What will you do if your marriage is in a season of worse, instead of better? How will you handle it? Granted, the bible declares that you can divorce when adultery has been committed and some may feel the need to leave, but if you and your spouse are determined together to make it work, DO JUST THAT! GOD HONORS MARRIAGE! God has the capacity, to heal and restore the broken hearted.

Then he said unto the disciples, It is impossible but that offenses will come; but woe unto him, through whom they come (Luke 17:1). What if the offense comes from the person you love most? What if it's a repeated offense? Can you carry a 70 x's 7 GRACE? Jesus said unto him, I say not unto thee, until seven times; but, until seventy times seven (Matthew 18:22). Can you continue to give of yourself? Can you still walk in the Love of God? And above all things have fervent charity among yourselves; for charity shall cover the multitude of sin. 1Peter 4:8. With tears in your eyes.....YES

On Bended knees.... YES.

Forgiveness heals the soul. Forgiveness releases you from consuming a root of bitterness that will impact every relationship in your life. The bitterness will turn into insecurity, the insecurity will turn into fear, and the fear will cripple your ability to grow in GOD.

Chapter Six
This is my Exodus..........

My norm was to sleep in at least until 10am on Saturday. This Saturday was quite different. I was up before 8am and began to pray, continually giving God his word, while not seeing any of it (I saw no manifestation of Gods promises, all I saw was my marriage getting worse, despite my efforts). My husband continued his relationship with the other woman and I felt like a fool for staying, serving, doing what God told me to do. The clarity, confirmation, and prayer strategies he gave me were nowhere to be found in my short term or long-term memory. The prayer he told me to pray had become dull and the authority initially attached was null and void. Void because I wanted God to move in my timing and not his.

The Prayer:

Every word curse and accusation against your word shall be made a lie! God I shall walk in my mandate to pray, cover, love, and support my husband. God thank you for revealing to me that maturity cannot exist until healing takes place. God thank you for the man of God that's going to rise up. God thank you that you will have his heart, and I am the woman to follow. No other word, suggestion, or opinion can sever that what you have put together. Let no man put us under. For in our house we shall pray together, study your word together, and serve you together. No longer will we be foreign to each other. But there will be a bond seared together by your blood. Thank you for telling me to shut up! God restore the brokenness in our children, restore the broken places in us. Teach us how to love, respect, and serve each other. God continue to reveal my authenticity unto my husband. God you asked me if I'm going to trust you or not. So God, I trust you. Not my friends, not the words and suggestions of others, but God I trust you. No generational curse will separate us. No word curse will prevail. We cancel the bloodline curse of jealousy, anxiety, being overwhelmed, not processing, not handling the gift of each other correctly, the controlling places and people, the bloodline is broken today! The curse is broken today! Shift our culture into the culture of you, not family, not friends, not others. Every strange woman and man we cancel their assignment right now. Every strange woman or man attempting communication will be cut off at the neck, and we suffocate the oxygen supply of the attack. Devil you will not have my marriage, my children, or my home. God you shall have it, you created it!!!!! God my husband will be the man you called him to be. The pastor's calling on his life will be fulfilled!!!!! We will walk-in your greatness, distinction, and authority!!!!

Later that morning, I began to scroll through social media and came across the Sunday's Best episode with Leandria Johnson, and Donald Lawrence and the Tri City Singers. I had listened to the song numerous times before, I cried numerous times before, but that Saturday morning. I felt a shaking, spiritually. I looked down, and as my hands trembled , I could feel God dealing with the parts of me that were afraid to be alone and lonely, the undisciplined parts of me that needed to "look" the part, the parts of me that shopped frivolously instead of being responsible and paying bills. The parts of me that allowed our home to almost go into foreclosure. The parts of me that did not care about having a balanced checkbook, or financial security, the parts of me that did not fully trust him. The parts of me that acted very unseemly and literally attempting to stab my husband and others.

Do you remember the knife my mom had? Yep, I didn't have her knife, but I had my own. That little girl was alive. The hurt was fire in my bones, and at all cost, whosoever hurt me was going to pay. I remember calling my pastor, admitting my faults, and her calmly saying, "You are human, and you are hurt. It will be ok. Read the book of Proverbs daily, and it will give you wisdom." Proverbs took me to a new place, and that's where my faith began to grow. She said, "When you read it, call out your name and your husband's name with the scripture." I did just that and after a few weeks, I could feel the sting begin to leave.

The parts of me that even though I prayed, deep within, I wanted the results I had in mind, the way I thought it should come, but God had a different idea and package for the delivery. These parts of me were destroying my marriage. THAT WAS THE DAY I BIRTHED FULL DELIVERANCE AND WALKED IN A LOVE LIKE NEVER BEFORE. NO MATTER HOW I WAS TREATED, MY HUSBAND BECAME

A PRIORITY AGAIN AND NOT AN OPTION. I WENT TO HIM IN AUTHENTICITY AND SINCERITY AND APOLOGIZED FOR EVERYTHING I DID TO HURT HIM.

On that day, I surrendered my will for God's will. On that day, God shattered every norm in my life, and my new norm became an intentional focus on my repentance, restoration and surrender instead of my outward desire to look the part and play the role that I had it all together. There was a soul work that needed to be done. There was a root that needed destroying. A root of bitterness, rejection, pride, rear, hostility, anger and destruction.

My healing, my restoration, my relationship with God. No one else and nothing else. That day I put on a new woman! That ye put off concerning the former conversation the old man, which is corrupt according to deceitful lust; And be renewed in the spirit of your mind; And that ye put on the new man, which after God is created in righteousness and true holiness Ephesians 4:22-24).

Today I ask, what is your Exodus Moment? What is God allowing you to birth out that was poisoning your spirit and spiritual growth? What is living and breathing in you that needs a depleted oxygen supply? I made the mistake of trusting God in my way. I trusted him until my patience ran out, and then I picked my problem back up and handled it my way. HOW WRONG IS THAT? MY NEED TO CONTROL EVERYTHING AND EVERYONE, CAUSED ME TO HOLD ON TO MY WILL UNKNOWINGLY.

The mistake taught me that when you are in covenant with God and your spouse, every decision you make effects everyone in your household, and my shoddy thinking was propped on the hinges of destroying everyone and everything around me. Bad times will shift you into a place of revenge if you are not in position to hear GOD.

God will change you before he changes the situation. Will you allow the change? Are you ready for what comes with and in the change? Change yields transformation. A real change shifts your soul. A real change delivers you from your will and replaces the desire of your soul with God's will. Transition is sometimes long and hard. Can you stand the pain? Will you allow your cross to cross the barriers of generational curses, bloodline curses, and word curses in your life? Generational curses of learned helplessness, impoverished mindsets, controlling spirits, divorce, and jealousy along with so many more will ruin lives, and separate you from the promises of God. Yes, they kill, steal, and destroy the good God placed in you. To break the curse, God has to break us.

"When you have been called to be the generational curse breaker for your family, the breaking starts with you."

Chapter Seven
Your Present Suffering

I don't want to give false hope (when it comes to trials and tribulations). During your transition in GOD, he will not speak always. There will be times where he requires you to STAND and his silence is louder than anything else. But in his silence, allow his word to speak. Meditate on things that are pure and holy (Philippians 4:8). Surround yourself with positive people, get rid of distractions (social media, music that taints your spirit, filthy conversation, explicit TV shows, e.g.) study the word of God, let the pages become life to your situation. May God's word be the words to your narrative. May God's word be the keeping power you need.

Strangely, God speaks to me in the most profound way in the shower. I will never forget the "morning after." The night before I was in a very angry space concerning a decision my husband made that impacted our family, the decision to leave home. I expressed my concern and feelings to him and told him that he punked out on his family. Was it nice to say? No. Did I sin? No. Was it disrespectful? Yes! You can be angry and sin not, while bringing offense at the same time. Be ye angry and sin not: let not the sun go down on your wrath (Ephesians 4:26).

The morning after God said to me, you can birth good and bad. In our PUSH to remain close to GOD, there are fleshly desires, attachments, generational curses, and just plain sinful natures

Picking Up The Pieces

that we carry. It takes GOD to birth those things out of us, so that he may live in us. What are you pushing out?????

Living within was a spirit of disrespect that made my husband cringe. That very thing needs to be birthed out of me. Spiritual birth can be delivering a new ministry or assignment, but it can also be the pushing out of the very thing that will separate you from GOD. What labor pains are you having? Sarah gave birth to a nation. Mary gave birth to a savior. Can God trust you with the same? Can God trust you with his fragile hearts?

After your baby is born, there is an afterbirth (Placenta) that must come out or the mother's life will be at risk due to serious infection or excessive blood loss. The purpose of the placenta is to provide oxygen to the baby and remove waste products from their blood. The oxygen is no longer needed once the baby has left the womb. A sac filled with waste is a breeding ground for stench, disease, and infection. Each stage in pregnancy has a purpose. The final labor pain or contraction is needed to push out the placenta. Hold fast, push out your placenta, allow God to get all of the bad out of you, to avoid unnecessary contamination of your new blood. When we accepted Christ, we're given a spiritual blood transfusion. Don't contaminate your new with the old. Behold he makes all things new. (Revelation 21:5).

PUSH: Persistent Understanding of Sacrifice on a Higher level.

I remember like it was yesterday, GOD said SHUT UP!! LOUD, BOLD, AND CLEAR!! In the middle of my stand for my marriage, I had to be quiet. In the middle of the hurt I felt,

I had to be quiet? Maybe I heard wrong. Maybe I missed something. NOPE, he said it again, SHUT UP! It felt like heavens doors closed and my mouth had been wired shut.

God became silent. I could feel him watching me. It was like every time I tried to speak anything pertaining to my marriage, he was standing over me waiting to gently slap my hand and give correction, while reminding me of what he told me to do. Maurice (my husband) would come home and say are you ok? All I could say was yes. I wanted to say soooooo much more!!! Being a very verbal woman, taught to say what you feel no matter who it hurts, I was devastated. My insides were boiling. I wanted to say so much, and could not! Could it be that my husband was in a place of pain himself, and one more word from me would push him over the edge? Could it be that God was showing me what I needed to work on? I didn't know, but what I did know was I was FURIOUS!

The quiet and the silence was debilitating. The silence killed the residue in me wanting to be in control. The residue that wanted to speak my peace and say what was right and wrong. BUT NOT SO, NOT THIS TIME. SILENCE SPOKE, SILENCE REIGNED, SILENCE WON. My will wanted to talk it out, explain, and fix it.... God's will wanted silence. No, I was not wrong for wanting to voice my hurt and my recognition of the pain I felt, but was it going to edify in the moment? I could hear my pastor saying, "This is not the time for that." "All things are lawful for me, but all things are not expedient: all things are lawful for me, but all things edify not" (1 Corinthians 10: 23).

What you feel and want to express may be valid, but is it useful in the moment? We must acknowledge God in all our ways.

Speaking at the wrong time and with the wrong words could have potentially ruined everything for me. The Bible tells us, For I reckon that the sufferings of this present time are not worthy to be compared with the glory that shall be revealed in us (Romans 8:18). God was getting the glory out of my silence. Healing was taking place in the midst of my silence. I could feel the wound in my heart begin to close. The cracks and crevices were being cleaned in the silence.

Many are the afflictions of the righteous, but the Lord delivers him from them all (Proverbs 34:19). The "many" can come like a rushing wind. But the rushing wind is no comparison to the east wind that God delivers. It's a wind of destruction that will annihilate your adversary. I will scatter them as with an east wind before the enemy; I will shew them the back, and not the face, in the day of their calamity (Jeremiah 18:17).

The many can come through work, family, friends, finances, your mindset, even the church. We must be strong in faith knowing if God allowed it, he will provide the endurance to go through it. Embrace your many. Embrace it by Acknowledging God in all of your ways and he will direct your path. In every fight, he provides favor. You are never alone. He will never leave you or forsake you. Cast your cares on him for he cares for you. God will always confirm his promises to us through his word.

"In the center of your many, lives your making."

Chapter Eight
God Meets Us Where We Are.....

During my season of offense God gave me instruction. The book of Ecclesiastes tells us that to everything there is a season. I found myself in the middle of a pruning season. Flowers such as roses go through a pruning season. There are 8 steps to this process. I was being pruned for the glory of God.

Step 1; Remaining leaves are removed. My normal dysfunction was being cut away. My need to be seen, heard, and respected. My desire to make my case known and repay those who hurt me. My innate passion to look the part, while being written off inside, all of it was being cut off.

Step 2. Start with the dead wood..... Boy was I dead. Dead to the things of God. I was living a life full of fleshly desires. Scripture tells us that we must crucify the flesh daily. I crucified my husband daily with words of rejection, pride, haughtiness, anger, deceit, and malice. I was full of poison. I needed to die, that Christ may live. I needed to start with me. May I become the change I want to see.

Step 3. Open the center of the plant. My heart and soul needed to receive the Agape Love of God. I needed to open the windows and doors of my heart and let God in. I received a triple bypass (Cardiac Surgery where the heart is opened and normal blood flow is restored to an obstructed coronary artery). In my case. I had three blockages. The father, son, and

Holy Ghost needed to enter in. I needed the heavenly trinity at every level.

Step 4. Remove any thin, weak growth. Needless to say I was thin in patience and weak in faith. I needed a reality check. My fruit of the spirit were not producing. I had no characteristics of God. Love, Joy, peace, longsuffering, gentleness, goodness, faith, meekness, and temperance. All of these attributes were foreign to me. They were null and void. My character portrayed the complete opposite and God was not pleased.

Step 5. Prune the remaining canes. After being broken into several pieces, all I had remaining was a broken heart that was now ready for God to mend. An exhausted soul that was now ready to thrive again. A broken spirit, that was ready to be filled by God.

Step 6: Seal the fresh cuts: My wounds were open and ready for the word of God to be a balm. Ready for the spirit of God to be the antibiotic to cure my infection. My pride had taken me down a street called fool, and I decided to park the bus right there and find a new route. Jesus became my navigation system. The fertilizer to my soil.

Step 7. Clean Up. We must clean up what we mess up. Through repentance and a heart that was godly sorrow, I apologized to my husband with everything in me. I had to make it right. There was no other option. My way failed. God's way is always right and I finally realized it. The process of cleaning up (for me, picking up the pieces) is not fun. You have to be determined. Your faith will be tried. You must have perseverance.

Step 8. Feed you Roses. I began eating God. Through worship every morning. I gave my heart to God. In worship, you embody Christ. In worship, he is pleased. We were created to worship. In worship your heart is open to receive, and God has room to deposit. God is a gentleman, he does not force himself on anyone, we must choose him, and choose to worship. Prayer and worship became my weapon, but that was not all!

God met me where I was. He is a complete God, his very name embodies everything that we need, but that does not eliminate our ordered works. James 2:20 says, Faith without works is dead. That means believing God can do it is not enough. We have a cross to carry. Every trial or test we endure, either God allows it or he causes it. Here are a few examples. He caused the Jesus to be led into the wilderness to be tempted by satan (Matthew 4:1). He allowed satan to consider and try Job (Job 1:6-8). This in itself is a reminder that God is with us in everything.

Our part is to search his scripture and apply it. There is nothing new under the sun, and his word is life to every circumstance if you apply it.

God tells us that offense is inevitable (Luke 17:1).

He gives us his fruit of the spirit, his character to possess,
(Hebrews 12: 1-3)

Picking Up The Pieces

He tells us that it is impossible to please him without faith
(Hebrews 11:1-6)

We are commanded to lay aside every weight that so easily beset us

(Hebrews 12: 1-3)

After I gained faith, acknowledged the offence, adapted his fruit of the spirit, and laid aside every weight, I can now take up my bed and walk

(John 5: 1-8).

God wants us to walk it out. He never promised it would be easy, but he did promise to be there with us. What are your directions in the word of God? How will you apply it?

To add, you may need an accountability partner, coach, or therapist to give you practical application along with the word. There is nothing wrong with maintaining your mental health. If you have found yourself stuck, or unable to move beyond your past trauma, a mental health professional may be able to assist you.

For heart issues we see a cardiologist, for stomach issues we see a gastroenterologist. Why not see a psychiatrist or psychologist for the brain? It's an organ as well. Dr. Anita Phillips says, "Prayer is a weapon, therapy is a strategy."

Life is hard. We sometimes get knocked off of our rocker. God will never leave us or forsake us. Acknowledge your journey, take Gods hand, and do the work needed to become whole again. Find what your "works" are, because your faith is dead without them.

Chapter Nine
Release is the Prerequisite to Restoration

Will you allow God to restore, rebuild, and reconnect the lost places in you? Will you relinquish control, trust God, and release your way? When we step in the way of God, we tie his hands and the angels assigned to our destiny are called to a halt. We must accept our wrong, surrender our will, and relinquish control of the situation. As we do this, we allow God to rest, rule, and abide in our lives at full capacity.

H.A.L.T........this acronym is used by psychologist, psychiatrist and life coaches worldwide. These 4 emotions are triggers for destructive behaviors if positive coping skills are not interjected and used to replace shoddy thinking.

H. Hungry

A. Angry

L. Lonely

T. Tired

What are you **HUNGRY** for? Feed your hunger with the word (Matthew 4:4). Man shall not live by bread alone, but every word that proceeds out of the mouth of God. My hunger was fueled by the need for my husband to make me happy. WRONG! As women we remember our childhood with Ken and Barbie. That's the beginning of the fairytale and the lie.

Picking Up The Pieces

No marriage is perfect every day and at some point, one will have to carry the other because both are rarely strong at the same time.

This topic came up at work and a coworker said I disagree, I'm the strong one. I went to her and explained her present situation and that her spouse was the strong one because he is taking the brunt of her frustrations during this season. She quickly agreed.

Weakness can come in several forms. As women we must remember when we are in our strong season, we don't get to choose how long we will get to be strong. Christ was strong for the world when he hung on the cross, we will never endure that. We often forget a wife is a ministry. You must be anointed with a grace to carry, build and encourage your spouse.

What makes you **ANGRY**? Be angry but sin not (Ephesians 4:26.). My anger became a root of bitterness as I focused on the rejection and hurt caused by the 2 men I loved the most. I became comfortable being the victim. I liked the attention I got when complaining about the bad instead of praising God for the moment. I was the center of attention and it was easier to have a pity party than accept the fact that my life is what I make it and I can't blame anyone for the hand I was dealt but I can make a decision to live a life purposed with destiny by GOD!

What are you **LONELY** for? "Be strong and of good courage, fear not, nor be afraid of them: for the Lord thy God, he it is that go with thee; he will not fail thee, nor forsake thee.

(Deuteronomy 31:6). I was lonely for acceptance and appreciation for what I did. In all efforts to make a home in my way, it failed. I was conceded and took no thought to how my husband felt or how my actions would impact him. My action left a reaction of loneliness. My actions left my husband feeling not needed, unsupported, and unequipped to lead his family.

What are you **TIRED** of? And let us not be weary in well doing: for in due season we shall reap, if we faint not (Galatians 6:9). I was beyond tired of being an option and not a priority, a second thought, tired of me and the children being the back seat crew BUT was my home welcoming and inviting? Did I make my husband want to come home, or run away because of my nagging? Did I belittle him in front of the children? YES. Did I cause the very thing I was tired of? YES. I SURE DID.

My brother, Darryl says, "It behooves you to listen to wisdom and instruction from the Lord." Ladies, it behooves you to lose yourself before you say I do, or you will be alone with yourself when your mate becomes tired. Discover your insecurities, lack, resentments, and downfalls. Allow God to remake and restore you. He will take a flawed woman and make her great in the sight of the man he has for her. Be humble. Hear God. Surrender you, and take on Christ.

Coupling prayer and therapy, counseling or coaching can only make you better. Find someone that can relate to you and your spouse. Every couple needs another couple capable of mentoring them into their next place. If you would like to apply biblical principles to your sessions, ensure that your therapist or coach is aware of that from the beginning. God ordained marriage so he must remain in every aspect of it. Marriage was ordained of God. It can only prosper when he is leading it.

Chapter Ten
The Threshing of the Wheat

When wheat goes through a threshing process its good portion is separated from the chaff. Completing the process by hand is very labor intense and takes an hour by hand for only one bushel.

In the hands of God, I had to endure (and still endure) my threshing. He needs my good for his glory. Piece by piece, hand by hand, hour by hour. Being stricken with hurt, beat down with guilt and shame, while proclaiming the will of God for your life is like a bushel of wheat before the threshing. Our chaff (bad) cannot be used to glorify God so he must come in and separate. It won't work if we are professing the power but only have a form of Godliness? Having a form of godliness, but denying the power thereof: from such turn away (2 Timothy 3:5). We must be real in our walk with God, only the truth will last. There is truth in God and knowing that he is able to do exceedingly and abundantly above all we may ask or think, but you must believe it. For it is impossible to please God without faith. (Ephesians 3:20 and Hebrews 11:6).

Your storms and trials reveal your core. For years my core was corrupt! Our core is made up of our will or God's will. The one you hunger for and feed more will survive in the famine. When temptation comes, the greater will rise. For his word is a lamp unto my feet, and a light unto my path (Psalm 119:105).

Picking Up The Pieces

I will never forget our couple's trip to Tennessee (5 hour drive). An argument brewed that lasted at least an hour between Maurice and I. Did I mention, I failed with flying colors time! My flesh was in full control. But thank God for Jesus, he loved me enough to correct me! His correction should be an ornament of grace around your neck. Embrace the correction. Don't allow your bad to spoil the good.

Destiny desires sacrifice. Your next place in God will require a sacrifice, but most of all obedience. Obedience is better than sacrifice. (1Samuel 15:22). I can remember telling God, "How long will I look like a fool for you." THAT WAS BOLD! THAT WAS THE LITTLE GIRL AGAIN! Sometimes we are required to do what is foolish to the world, but sane to God. For the bible tells us that his ways and thoughts are not ours. (Isaiah 55:8).

Husbands are to love their wife as Christ loves the church, he died for us. Women are to be a help meet, to love and respect their husband. Marriage is a representation of Christ and the church. He is the groom and we are the bride. Reflect: how are you treating your groom in heaven? It will reflect on how you treat your groom on earth.

Yolanda Roary

Chapter Eleven
The Dry Wood Factor

Every fire needs a piece of dry wood to keep the flames alive. Every person needs someone pouring into them, keeping them in a posture of hearing and receiving from God. We will have seasons where we feel like giving up, and overwhelming feelings where we have no strength. In the boxing ring, the fighters tap out for encouragement, and small wounds are tended to. Afterwards, they go back in the ring, ready for the win! Where we are weak, that's when God is strong.

In my introduction, I spoke of the two women in my life that were midwives and dry wood to my fire. It is imperative that we find strong Godly women in our life to encourage us in GOD, pray with us, and hold us accountable. I can remember my friend Sonya telling me, "Yolanda, you know better!" What you are doing is not right! I ignored her.

Have you ever put wood on a fire that was not hot enough? The fire lacked stirring that circulated heat, which causes the ambers to catch new wood afire? That's where I was spiritually. I was not stirring my own fire so when Sonya stepped in, I was too wet with my own desires, but thank God for people being assigned to your destiny, whether you're ready or not, they are in a place to stay right there and pray you through until you get it. She has been by my side daily. Holding me accountable for every word and deed. I remember my PLE Co-leader and mentor, Shemekka telling me, "We hold our bleeding wounds, while bandaging others." That's what Sonya did for me. I am forever grateful for the long talks, patience and love she shared with me during my season of stubbornness.

Now Crystal was my "thug" midwife. She experienced a lot in life before surrendering to God and it's not easy to get over on her. She can discern a trickster from a mile away. She is accountable for my boldness in GOD. Her spirit gave me the righteous indignation to put satan in his place! She will stop, drop, and pray in a hot minute! She would say, "You can get right, or get left." So many times she prayed me through rough places. So many times she would call, and her words would be right on time, just what I needed to fight a little harder.

For every piece of dry wood, every word, prayer, and petition to God on my behalf, I am grateful.

Lastly, I encourage all of you, find the dry wood in your life. Someone who will hold you accountable, show you the way, and will fight satan for you when you can't. It is imperative that the people in your corner, want your marriage to succeed as much as you do. Naysayers, and those who do not understand God's will for your life will give you wood, but it won't be dry. Your fire will remain out when your wood is not mature enough to stand the test.

Level up in you friendships. A true friend will understand when God has placed you in a wilderness for a season, and will not encourage you to leave, but instead, they will pray you through. (Matthew 4:1).

For God will use every part of us for his glory!!!!! Iron sharpeneth iron; so a man sharpeneth the countenance of his friend (Proverbs 27:17).

Chapter Twelve
Choose the Mandate and Not the Mess

In the consulting world, traveling became the norm. God never failed to amaze me. Every trip taken with the Institute for Healthcare Improvement was ministry. Each destination came prepared with a soul and God prepared me to give a word of encouragement and hope. Being a vessel for the master has kept me humble and in a place to know that no matter where I am, it's for him to get the glory!

Distractions are made of MESS......They come to rid your focus of God and shift your thought process into a place of assumption and negativity. The mess can come through a phone call, a text, a social media post, even a friend or family member.

Away on a business trip, I entertained a phone call that was full of worldly truth but not Godly truth when it came to my situation. God had other plans for me and those plans were the complete opposite of what the world would consider normal or sane. I was told that it would be best to leave my husband, and I needed to admit that he was not the one God had for me. Scripture tells us to Hear counsel, and receive instruction, that thou mayest be wise in the latter end (Proverbs 19:20). We must be careful, we must be wise. All counsel may not be appropriate for your season, or place in God. It is imperative that we acknowledge God in all of our ways.

Was some type of plan being devised? Were there intimate conversations I knew nothing about concerning my marriage? I must admit, I became tearful, and had to talk to myself, while praying through it. But in my core, I knew something just wasn't right. Was their truth in some of her sayings? Those truths could not be denied, but those truths were to be made a lie with Gods word. They were worldly truths that cannot and will not stand against God's truth and his direction and instruction for my life.

Feelings overcame me with sadness, and anger, as fear rushed inside of me, but no words formed. "Wherefore, my beloved brethren, let every man be swift to hear, slow to speak, slow to wrath." (James 1:19). Those closest to us often have our best intention at heart, but what if that intention is the complete opposite of the mandate God has placed upon our lives, and where God wants you in that season of your life. What if their best intention will deliver us into disobedience? The Bible tells us that obedience is better than sacrifice.

Hearing the wrong voice of instruction at the wrong time becomes a breeding ground for spiritual miscarriage and abortion. When God gives instruction that will lead us into deliverance and destiny, it will be the complete opposite of what looks natural and sane to the world. For nevertheless, his will be done. What is in the center of your nevertheless? Your nevertheless may come with pain, sacrifice, loss, and suffering. We are groomed by the process of making it through our "nevertheless". As Christ waited and prayed, he told God, nevertheless, thy will be done. He asked God to take away the bitter cup, but he knew he had a purpose to fulfil. Don't abort your purpose for anyone.

God reminded me that I had a task at hand and ministry was right around the corner and if I didn't adhere to my mandate of intercession, this mess in the moment would hinder me from hearing God in the midst of my praying. My spirit leaped in peace. And the peace of God, which surpasses all understanding, shall keep your hearts and mind through Christ Jesus (Philippians 4:7). I immediately reminded the caller of the mandate on my life from God and that I would rather look like a fool for God than be right in the eyes of man.

"The eyes of man will lead you astray, the eyes of God will deliver you straight way."

It didn't stop there. The devil doesn't give up that easy. Immediately after hanging up, the devil began to speaking to me, CONSTANTLY. I needed to get in the face of GOD and quickly. I got to my hotel and immediately went into prayer and worship. God spoke, encouraged, and freed me from the weight. It was if the burden was lifted in midair. My worship created a space for God to move every burden. My worship created space for me to hear God speak. I was free from the weight that tried to attach itself.

No Mess Is Greater Than My Messiah!!!

I told the devil he was the biggest fool to try and stop what God ordained me to do! The weather was perfect, view was amazing and I could feel God in the wind. Each morning and night for 3 days I sat there and God spoke. He gave clarity in difficult situations, prayer strategies, and confirmation of what he was going to do in my family, mainly my marriage. Needless to say my business partner arrived, I was able to hear God, pray the specific prayer into her life and God moved! If the mess of the moment would have distracted me, my business partner would not have received what she needed from God in the moment because I would not have been in place to give it. God would have chosen someone else to deliver his package. May I always be in a place where God can use me.

Yolanda Roary

Chapter Thirteen
The Transformation

I can remember vividly going upstairs to search my sons' room to check on him. He was on punishment for a fight in school that resulted in his suspension. I walked in the room, at the sight of clothes everywhere, old food, drinks, cups, just disaster. I began screaming and telling him that he knew better and the room was a mess, filthy and stink. The look of disgust on his face was threatening. It offended me on all levels and I made him aware that his disrespect would not be tolerated.

Before my eyes, he transformed into his dad at the age of 15. His shoulders dropped; his face was engulfed with sadness. And his countenance displayed no hope at all. No will, no desire to do better, depressed with the weight that was not his to carry. He was stripped of his humanity, stripped his self-esteem, stripped of his ability to be a normal teenager. I imposed my fears on him.

We suffocate the hope in our children by smuggling it with our fears, regrets, and childhood experiences. This moment had a 2-edged sword. God also showed me the hurt inside of my husband. The places in him that need to be loved and not scorned. The things that needed to be released.

For my son, God allowed me to see his need to have a voice, the need to be his true and authentic self, the need to be an innocent child, without carrying the burden of adulthood. The need to be trained as a child, and not expected to do and be an adult. That was the first time God allowed me to experience a spiritual transformation and I will never forget it. That moment reminds me of the broken girl inside of me, and the importance of me not breaking or bleeding on my children with my regrets, and lack of healing from my childhood neglect.

"Release is the prerequisite to Restoration."

If we do not release our past into the hands of a God equipped to handle it, we will never be restored. Holding on to the thing that hurt us, and its invisible, crippling effect, has the ability to demolish our lives and those closest to us. It prevents us from being who God called us to be, and walking in his purpose and destiny for our lives. This very thing happens to the children we break repeatedly because we are too prideful to release and be restored. We are too prideful to do the work required to become whole. To prideful to experience the pain. To face it, feel it, and fix it…naturally and spiritually. But without faith it is impossible to please him: for he is a rewarder of them who diligently seek him (Hebrews 11:6). Seek ye first the kingdom of God and all his righteousness, and all these things will be added unto you (Matthew 6:33). Look in the mirror, see all of you, not just the outside that smells good, looks good, and sounds good. Dig deep…find the boy or girl beaten down with neglect, lack of love, encouragement, and support. Find the child beneath it all. Remove the mask, and allow God to meet you face to face.

"When you discover what's hidden beneath the rubble of your past, the world looks different. You no longer make those around you a victim and you are no longer a victim to yourself."

Yolanda Roary

Chapter Fourteen
Broken to keep Breaking

In the midst of my surrendering, God left nothing untouched. My 3 children were suffering because of my disobedience. When parents are out of order, their negligence to obey becomes a feeding source to a household of chaos. While I was busy blaming my husband, what were my faults? The very sin that separated me became the covering that separated my children. All 3 of my children began acting out. My humble daughter grew bold and smart at the mouth (wonder where she got that from??) My smart 9-year-old began talking back and was full of anger, while my 15-year-old was lost and alone.

Generational curses, bloodline curses, and word curses are real! We must make an INTENTIONAL decision to break it! When you are mandated by God to be the breaker for your family, it will not be easy, don't be mistaken. Satan will attack everything attached to you. He is on the line, seeking to kill, steal, and destroy everything good thing God bestowed upon you!!! Everything you need, God has already placed inside of you. But you cannot access it tied up in your desires. It's found in the word of God, it's found in his presence, it's found in fasting, you must crucify your flesh in order to hear God CLEARLY. Distractions must be cut off, God will not fight for your attention. All of you must come to him. I can hear my pastor telling me to grow up! She said, "When will you think about the children God has given you, Get over yourself!" With boldness she spoke, and I could hear God clearly, I could hear the quickening and intensity in her words. I could hear the call for action.

God began to deal with me about a broken cycle. My husband was raised by a single mother and so was I. A woman can only teach a boy so much. She is not a man and cannot teach him to be a man. The love, encouragement, and security a man gives his daughter, a woman cannot give. When we become consumed with self, but not our spiritual selves, we break those attached to us, our children. My selfishness became a stronghold that would eventually separate my family, break them, and eventually breed broken men and women...the cycle repeats. Every child needs guidance, direction, and correction, but just as much, they need encouragement, and validation from their parents. Children are to be trained, not told.

We are given clear instruction in the word of God. Train up a child in the way he should go: and when he is old, he will not depart from it (Proverbs 22: 6). Google defines Train: teach (a person or animal) a particular skill or type of behavior through practice and instruction over a period of time. I admit, my version of training was point and tell. Rarely did I show what I was asking them to do, and when it was done wrong, I yelled, told them they knew better, and expected them to make it right. Scarce was the amount of thanks and appreciation I gave. I treated my children as adults, the very thing they were not. As a result of our brokenness and the lack of desire to become whole and healed in God we are bleeding on our children and they are drowning not only in their blood, but by our blood that has covered them.

In the midst of all of the chaos and spiritual error, I started a consulting and coaching firm. With a desire to see people made whole and businesses thrive without bias, I began consulting and coaching. I was saving the world while losing my family. Until I got a wakeup call from heaven....God said, "You cannot correct and strategize the lives and businesses of those around you and your home is out of order, charity starts at home!" I had to apologize to my children and my husband for my mistake, for the inner drive inside of me that caused me to selfishly leave them behind. God is a God of decency and order. But if any provide not for his own, and especially for those of his own house, he hath denied the faith, and is worse than an infidel (1 Timothy 5:8). Let all things be done decently and in order (1 Corinthians 14:40).

In the book of Ruth Chapter 1 verse 16 she tells Naomi these things after losing her husband, "Do not urge me to leave you, or to return from following you. For where you will go, and where you lodge I will lodge."

Where can our children go, where will they stay, if not in the bosom of their parents? Ruth is speaking to her mother in-law. In her words, she vividly expresses the inner most feelings after being left alone with nothing and no one, so she pleads with Naomi. That is the alone our children feel when we do not handle them as a child, and we set expectations for them that their adolescent mind cannot reach or possibly comprehend. This is felt when we are unaware that our brokenness is breaking them.

Healing had to take place in me, so that my children would be healed. God asked me a few questions. Will the generational curse be broken with you? Or will you continue being a victim? Will you allow me to take your broken places and make you whole in order to raise whole children who will become effective men and women in the kingdom? Now that I am picking up the pieces to a mended relationship with my children. I can walk in wholeness and a victory that only comes from God.

This process is like any other, it will take time. These pieces will need to be picked up carefully, for children are fragile beings, easily broken if not handled properly. But I will never forget. I can do all things through Christ which strengthens me (Philippians 4:13). I heard God loud and clear, every question!

There was another healing in me that screamed deep within my valley, my low place. I was still bothered by past experiences with my husband. Things that I walk in forgiveness with, but still bleed with hurt and the residue of the pain it caused. What can I do about it? Can I change the situation/s? Or maybe the question should be, Can I change me? Yes, there is a change in me. God revealed the issue by exposing an issue. God uses us according to his will and way. We do not get the liberty of choosing how he equips us to be used for his glory. When we tell God use me, it's best to know what you're asking because anything used has wear and tear!

I was not ready to accept the wear and tear on my heart, until I understood the spiritual circumcision of the heart needed to love Gods people unconditionally.

When I think of Christ as he carried his cross, endured a beating, a whipping, a flogging, a hanging, a piercing in his side and thorns on his head. What position was his heart in? Could it be that it was consumed with wear and tear from the pain of rejection, beating and crucifixion, but overcome with love??? God wants us to be overcome with his love!

"Heal, so that when triggers are present, you remain balanced."

Will you be the one? Can God trust you to be the vessel to go against the order of the world, and walk in total surrender to his will? Will you Stand on the line of righteousness, will you stay in the battle? Will you deny you? Will you give God total access?

"Find your balance in God, he is a just weight."

Chapter Fifteen
The Beginning of a New Ending

Some of my pieces are heavy, and exhausting. The pain that comes with carrying them can be excruciating, but the freedom of allowing God to take them and handle them at his discretion is liberating. Giving him free reign with the parts and pieces of me that can destroy a life has released me from the burden of perfection. I am now free from finding the perfect mask for the masquerade ball of life. My love for God covers a multitude of sin and fault. My love for God revealed that we all have sinned and fall short of the glory of God. My love for God revealed that I am not in control of another man's deliverance, not even my own. But I am in control of how I engage the process of my deliverance. I'm in control of whether or not I want the deliverance. Jesus is the navigator, he guides every stop, turn, yield and go.

I invite you today, take inventory of your pieces, allow God to guide your hand as you pick them up. None of us are perfect, God is a forgiving God. He loves you like he loves me. There is nothing in your past that's too heavy or big for God. Give it to him today. Surrender today. God is waiting at your cross road.

The stop sign is signaling you to end, so God may begin! If you need a coach or counselor to assist you in processing you scars, wounds, and the pain of your past, please do so. Don't become stagnant. Sometimes we need a cocktail of practical and spiritual to be successful and overcome the enemy!

Love, for it covers a multitude of sin and fault (1 Peter 4:8).

We all have sinned and come short of the glory of God (Romans 3:23).

At my crossroad are many broken pieces, but now, after yielding and surrendering to the voice of God , those pieces that were meant to destroy me, have made me into a better woman.

My pieces hold my future.

My pieces hold my past.

My pieces hold my destiny.

As I pick them up one by one, God is right beside me, waiting, to turn all of them into a masterpiece. The good, the bad, and the ugly.

Earlier, I mentioned finding a counselor, coach or mentor to help you when your marriage seems like it is failing:

Married 4 Real (www.married4Real.com): God allowed my husband and I to enroll in Mentorship with (M4R) Married 4 Real. LeTroy and Christina Brown are God sent with an anointing to break yokes off of marriages under attack. Enrolling into their program was the best thing we could have done. We see a change in each other and we have a hope and expected end. We have a NEW Marriage! We have learned how to navigate God's word and apply it to our marriage and our struggles. This is the beginning of our new ending.

Picking Up The Pieces

Again, find counsel for your marriage, find accountability, but most of all FIND GOD IN THE MARRIAGE AGAIN!

The trajectory of our marriage changed!!!! Through biblical principles and practical application, Christina and Letroy (Founders of M4R) ministered to us, while living a godly example of what a Kingdom marriage should be and look like. Again, find mentorship for your marriage, it will save the life of your marriage. I can now speak that wherever we go, God will get the Glory, and his purpose shall be revealed!

I now know what it means to serve, to sacrifice, and to be a wife and a help meet. Although beaten by the weight of disappointment, pain, hurt, anger, and fear, I can carry my cross. I pray for my husband daily. I encourage him. I manage our finances the right way, and when I want to stray, I go to my husband to reel me back in. I no longer shop when I'm angry. I go the extra mile for him. I treat him with respect. No longer do I withhold sexual intimacy from my husband because I did not get my way or I felt he handled me wrong. I was out of order, but by the grace of God, my husband can now rest in me. To be honest, I am still learning this new creature god has created in me, but I am loving her! She is amazing! The God I serve is a wonder!

My journey is not over, this is just the beginning. It ended with me and began in God.

I pray that the sharing of this season in my life, my marriage, my childhood, and my soul has blessed you, but most of all encouraged you to draw closer to God.

Be Blessed.

Yolanda Roary

Prayer of Salvation

To my readers that have made the decision to accept Christ as your personal savior…..CONGRATULATIONS!!!!!

You are about to embark on the greatest journey of your life. You will have good and bad, but know that God is right there with you all the way and he will never leave you or forsake you!

For God so loved the world that he gave his only begotten son, and whosoever believeth in him shall not perish but have everlasting life….John 3:16

It's a simple prayer…….

Say it aloud, for your words have power…..

Father in the name of Jesus, I ask for forgiveness of all of my sins, and I accept you as my Lord and Savior today. I believe that your son Jesus dies for my sins. Today, guide me, help me to follow you and live for you. In Jesus name, Amen

You did it! You are saved!!!! You are a child of God!!!

I recommend you find a spiritual mother or father. Attend a church that gives you the word of God and ministers to your spirit. Go to bible study and Sunday School, the more of God's word you know, the better you will be.

Surround yourself with likeminded people. Avoid atmospheres that house habits you are trying to break. Find an accountability partner. Do not be afraid to seek a coach or psychiatrist for ways to deal with issues that are deep rooted

Picking Up The Pieces

and impact your life daily. There is nothing wrong with prayer and therapy. That is a myth. Prayer will reveal and therapy will help you heal!

Be sure your therapist or coach understands your new place in GOD*

Remember this day, for it is your spiritual birthday.

                Happy Birthday!!!!

Strategy:

When you make a decision to wage war against the enemy and take our life back, you must have a strategy. Satan is very tactical and you must be one step ahead.

Put on the whole armor of God that you may be able to stand against the wiles of the devil.....Ephesians 6:11

Your helmet of salvation must be secure......A helmet covers your head. It's protection. Christ wore a crown of thorns symbolizing the impact of our thoughts on our lives. If satan can control your thoughts, he can control your life. And be not conformed to this world: but be ye transformed by the renewing of your mind, that ye may prove what is that good, and acceptable, and perfect, will of God (Romans 12:2).

A double minded man is unstable in all his ways (James 1:8). Be stable in your thoughts, when temptation comes, you have the power to cast down imaginations and every high thing that exalteth itself against the knowledge of God, an bringing into captivity every thought to the obedience of Christ (2 Corbin. 10:5).

The Breastplate of Righteousness.....A Breast plate protects your major organs. In the spirit, it protects you from the fiery darts of the enemy. HIs words, his attacks, his set ups, and plans to destroy your life.

Your shield of Faith.....The shield is portable. The spiritual faith in your shield means you are equipped with NOW

Picking Up The Pieces

FAITH…..The substance of things hoped for and the evidence of things not seen (Hebrews 11:1). So no matter where you end up, your faith can deliver you. It moves with you! Your now faith will move mountains!

Your loins are gird with the belt of truth……And ye shall know the truth, and the truth shall make you free…..John 8:32. Everything we have lived and experience may not be good, but its truth will free us!

You have a Sword of the Sprit……the power of God's word and spirit can take down any demonic force or attack of the enemy. For the word of God is quick, and powerful, and sharper than any two edged sword, piercing even to the dividing asunder of soul and spirit, and of joins and marrow, and is a discerner of the thoughts and intent of the heart (Hebrews 4:12)

Your feet are shod with the preparation of the gospel. The steps of a righteous man are ordered by God, and he delighteth in his way (Psalms 37:23). Allow God to guide and direct you. His will and way are higher than yours. Accept his path for your life.

Prayer is the master weapon in war but it will not take you through the door to your destiny. You must walk through it. The woman with the issue of blood pressed her way through a crowd. The lame man had to take his bed and walk……You must Get to Jesus.

Prayer coupled with the word of GOD will increase your faith. Success is inevitable without prayer, the word, and relationship. They are a 3 fold cord. They bring you into complete union with God.

Worship is an extension. It's your secret place. There your troubles can't go, your burdens can not tarry in worship. When you worship, you tell God who he is, you reverence his splendor and holiness.

Your praise tells God thank you for the good and bad. You acknowledge God and his works in every situation. We were made to praise him!

Praise, Worship, Pray, Read, and Relationship!!!!

I will not lead you in false word.....some things will only come through fasting and prayer. The place I am in, and the deliverance that I now hold came through sacrifice and the crucifying of my flesh. Killing your flesh (fasting) gives you a spiritual keenness and discernment that will never be accomplished in the natural.

****Seek God on how to fast, medical conditions etc., may surface the need to fast differently***

May you be blessed as your pieces give you peace.

www.ingramcontent.com/pod-product-compliance
Lightning Source LLC
Chambersburg PA
CBHW050918160426
43194CB00011B/2462